Personal
Prayer
Notebook

John C. Souter

Tyndale House Publishers, Inc.
Wheaton, Illinois

Coverdale House Publishers, Ltd.
Eastbourne, England

Fifth printing, Tyndale House edition, October 1981
Personal Prayer Notebook
ISBN 0-8423-4819-0, paper
Copyright © 1974 by John C. Souter
Originally published by World Thrust Inc.
This Tyndale House edition published with permission of
World Thrust Inc.

Contents

Introduction

You probably picked up this book because you desire to improve your prayer life. Read the following instructions carefully, and you will not be disappointed. The *Personal Prayer Notebook* is designed as a tool to help Christians like you develop a deep, balanced, and consistent prayer life. Let it organize your prayer life on a daily basis. God wants to open a whole new world of answered prayer for you.

1

Purpose

Much of our fruitlessness in prayer is caused by not knowing our purpose. Prayer, essentially, is the expression of the human heart in conversation with God. It is intimate dialogue with the Creator.

Prayer's ultimate purpose, like that of the Christian life itself, is to know God and become like Him. When we realize that this is our goal, we will stop dwelling on our problems and start dwelling on God.

Prayer was never meant to be a spiritual answering service. God can give us everything we have ever wanted, but He knows human nature too well for that. We have missed the point until we realize we are praying, not for things, but *to be*, what God wants us to be. Things will come later, as our desires become more in tune with God's Spirit.

2

Consistency

How many times have you climbed into bed at night realizing you had not talked to the Lord all day? You probably spoke a few meaningful sentences to God before falling to sleep, but somehow you still possessed a sense of guilt over your failure to spend quality time with the Lord.

Most Christians believe in prayer. You believe in it or this book wouldn't be in your hands. But belief and practice can be two different things. God deserves more of our time and attention than short fleeting utterances throughout the day. He desires and deserves a quality quiet time in which our attention is solely focused on Him.

If you want a dynamic and successful prayer life, you must develop daily consistency. Jesus taught a parable on prayer to His disciples in Luke 18 "to show that at all times they ought to pray and not to lose heart."

If you do not have a consistent prayer time, you need one. Right now, before you read any further, make a commitment to God that by His power you want a regular quiet time every day. Ask Him to give you both the power and desire to meet that commitment.

To remind yourself of this decision, write your promise on the first page of the Prayer Diary. This notebook is designed to help you stay faithful. The Prayer Diary has boxes next to each day's date to measure your consistency.

3

Helps

To aid in establishing a consistent and meaningful quiet time, schedule a regular hour each day when you will meet God. Look for the best possible time for this moment with God. Know exactly what time you plan to start praying, and as the time approaches, hurry to keep your appointment with the Father.

Choose a specific place where you can pray without interruption. Let your family know where this location is and when you will be there. If necessary, take the telephone off the hook to avoid interruptions.

Sometimes when you pray, unfinished tasks will come to mind. Don't fight these impulses. Write down each task so it can be taken care of when you finish praying. If a friend you have offended comes to mind, contact him immediately after your quiet time to ask forgiveness. A clear conscience is essential for a powerful prayer life.

Prayer is a spontaneous flowing of love and feeling toward God. But guard against being so "loose" you do not discipline yourself for godliness. Take the extra effort to write down your feelings in the prayer diary. Honestly record both your high and low moments. The discipline of writing things down will free your mind from unnecessary clutter, record your spiritual progress, and aid you in thinking through your commitments to God.

You will be using a different prayer list each day of the week so that every day's prayer task should be an exciting challenge. But if your quiet time becomes a meaningless routine which you are doing only out of a sense of obligation, then it is time to reexamine your spiritual life. Don't ever be satisfied with a routine relationship with the Father. Ask Him to motivate you to greater excitement.

When you're tired, pray with your eyes open. When you're offering personal confession, you might beseech God from your knees. When you are excited, walk around the room. Pray standing, sitting, or lying down. Pray silently or out loud. You might even try singing to God. Your mind and body are inseparably connected, so let your physical position suit your mood and increase your devotion.

Before you begin your quiet time, take a look into God's heart by studying His Word. The Bible is a mirror which will reveal things in your life which need to be changed. The *Personal Bible Study Notebook* can help in this study time.

4

Balance

It is very easy to become unbalanced in our prayers. In the Bible, five different activities compose the complete essence of prayer. This notebook will help you maintain balance in these areas.

Adoration/Worship

Adoration is the praise of God because of His greatness and goodness. It is the chief duty of man to glorify God. We glorify Him more by worship than by any other means. Worship is absolutely necessary if we are to live a happy Christian life. God wants it more than any other thing.

Your worship is not confined to any building. Jesus made that clear in John 4. You are the temple of God (1 Corinthians 6:19, 20) and as such it is very fitting for you to offer up adoration in your own quiet time.

When you worship, praise God for who He is. Write a psalm of praise like David. Focus on God's holy character and attributes. Tell Him how much you love Him. Glory in His greatness and goodness by giving all of yourself.

Thanksgiving

Thanksgiving is to be grateful, not only for the gifts of God, but for the Giver. The word means grateful, gracious, agreeable, and thankful.

"In everything give thanks, for this is the will of God in Christ Jesus concerning you" (1 Thessalonians 5:18). You must realize that God has allowed whatever happens to you. God lets things happen so that He may receive glory in the end. When you thank God for *everything*, as He commands, God will glorify Himself and all things will work together for your good (Romans 8:28).

1. Thank God when you wake. (Psalm 7:15; 118:24.)

2. Thank God about everything. (1 Thessalonians 5:18; Ephesians 5:20.)

3. Thank God when things look bad. Giving thanks is vocalized

faith. Faith never dwells on the problem; it anticipates great things. (Mark 4:36-40; 11:22-24.)

4. Thank God when you don't want to. Make the sacrifice of offering praise. (Hebrews 13:15; Psalm 116:17.)

5. Thank God when you find yourself in the midst of sin. Give thanks for His forgiveness. (1 Corinthians 10:13; 1 John 1:9; Philippians 3:13, 14.)

Confession

After you accepted Christ's sacrifice for your sin, you were forgiven. But you still walk in a sinful world and need some provision for daily sin. Confession is God's remedy for this problem.

Confession comes only after you realize you have sinned. It is the act of agreeing with God that you are sinful. God is more interested that you deal with the rebellion which causes sinful acts than He is in your listing offenses one by one. He does not want you to dwell on your imperfectness, He wants you to meditate on His Word and dwell on the good and pure things in life. (James 1:25; Joshua 1:8; Philippians 4:8.)

When you offer confession you receive release from the burden of guilt feelings that plagues you. But confession was never meant to be an enjoyable experience. The pain of exposing yourself, without anything to hide behind, causes you to become concerned about recurring rebellion. It is only as you become concerned that God can show you how to sin less.

Intercession

Intercession is the act of praying for the needs of others. We must always remember it is our duty to help others get what they need, not necessarily what they want. When we pray for the needs of others, we become involved in their lives. (James 5:16; Philippians 2:2-4.)

God is not willing that any man should perish. He wants us to be as concerned about the lost as He is (Matthew 18:12, 13). For this reason we are told to pray for non-Christians (1 Timothy 2:1-4). Every Christian must have several non-Christians for whom he labors before God's throne.

When you pray for non-Christians, your biggest problem will be that you will see little fruit. It will be easy to grow weary of the task. Two things will help you persevere—praying weekly (realizing this is a long-term request), and praying with faith-sized requests.

Praying for someone to make a decision for Christ is like trying to jump up a flight of stairs. You get to the top by using the steps, not jumping. So when you desire the salvation of a friend you should pray them into the Kingdom in smaller steps. As each of these prayer steps is reached your faith in the task will be greatly encouraged.

Petition

Petition is making requests for our own needs. We are told to cast all our cares on Christ because He cares for us (1 Peter 5:7). Petition probably fills our quiet time more than any other prayer activity because our own needs are always present.

It is in the area of personal petitions that you will need to exercise the greatest amount of discipline and control. You must be certain that you do not ask for things for selfish reasons. You must also be careful that you do not get impatient and "get ahead" of God's time table.

5

Answers

God delights in answering the prayers of His people, but before He will grant your requests, you must ask for the right things in the right ways.

First, you must pray in or through the Spirit's power (Ephesians 6:18). To be in the Spirit's control there must be no unconfessed sin in your life (Psalm 66:18). When you try to run your own life, God's power is short-circuited. The Holy Spirit wants to fill you (Ephesians 5:18), but before He can take control you must yield your will to Him. Real mountain-moving prayer answers will never come until God is daily put on the throne of your life.

Second, you will never receive any answer to a request that is not according to God's will (1 John 5:14, 15). You must know, then, how to determine what His will is. God's will is always consistent with His Word. The more you know about what the Bible teaches the more likely it is that you will ask for things in line with His will. Study your Bible faithfully to learn the mind of God.

God's will is always in your best interests. He knows that some good things are really not the best for you. He judges the thoughts and intentions of your heart (Hebrews 4:12, 13; James 4:3) and does not give selfish desires.

If you talk to someone on the phone often, you can recognize his voice easily. Talk to God on a regular and intimate basis and soon you will recognize His voice too. He speaks through the "still small voice," that overwhelming sense of peace or lack of it. Colossians 3:15 says, "Let the peace of Christ rule in your heart." Learn to be sensitive to God's leading. Once He has revealed His will by giving peace, you can begin praying with fervor.

Finally, Jesus emphasized the importance of faith in receiving answers. He dramatized the need for totally believing God in several parables (Luke 11:5-13; 18:1-8). He revealed that persistence is closely connected with the kind of faith that does not waver or doubt (James 1:6, 7). It tells God you believe in His power to answer. It tells Him you know His answering is only a matter of time.

Faith has a way of growing. Every time God gives a positive answer to one of your prayers your faith will grow a little larger. The Answered Prayer section at the back of this book will record these spiritual victories and give greater opportunities to praise the Lord.

6

Organization

This notebook will help you pray "decently and in order." But don't let its organization and structure limit your time with God. If you desire to use more than one day's list, feel free to do so. The lists are designed to expand, not limit your horizons. Some days you may want to pray through all seven lists to stimulate your love-relationship with the Lord.

Begin your quiet time each day by looking up the day's prayer list. Once you have prayed over that list, turn to the Prayer Diary.

SUNDAY Adoration/Worship

Purpose—to recognize who God is and give Him honor and worship.

How to Begin—concentrate on God's nature. Praise Him for all that He is. It is a good idea to read some psalm of praise before you begin your worship time. It should take two to four prayer times to exhaust the spaces provided on this form. After you have filled all the blanks, move on to another form.

MONDAY Intercession/Non-Christians

Purpose—to pray non-Christians into God's family step by step.

How to Begin—write down the name of a non-Christian friend or loved one. (It is a good idea to choose people you see often.) Pray step by step for his or her salvation. Each step should be within the grasp of your faith. Pray for small things you believe God will give, like: an opportunity to talk to the friend about Christ, his responsiveness to spiritual things, his contact with other Christians, etc. God will answer step by step, often through your own personal witness.

TUESDAY Thanksgiving

Purpose—to thank God for the many good things He has done and will do.

How to Begin—as you offer thanksgiving to God, list specific things. Take a long look at all the many blessings God has showered on you. Do your best to cultivate a grateful spirit through this spiritual exercise. When you have used all the blanks, move on to other thanksgiving sheets.

WEDNESDAY Intercession/Missions
Purpose—to prayerfully support your missionaries and develop a consciousness of their needs.

How to Begin—select several missionaries. To obtain adequate information about them and their families, you may have to write a few letters. Prayer meeting is an excellent time to learn these facts. Remember to be concerned about the whole missionary family and their needs. Pray for your pastor in this section.

THURSDAY Intercession/Christians
Purpose—to bring the personal needs of your Christian friends before God.

How to Begin—write down the names of several Christians who have specific needs. Record each request and the date you begin asking—you will need to keep in touch with these people to discover how God answers. When you receive an answer, cross out that section on your list so you won't spend needless time over an answered item.

FRIDAY Personal Confession
Purpose—to confess and forsake those areas of your life which are inconsistent with God's Word and to focus upon the kind of character God wants you to develop.

How to Begin—this sheet calls attention to the areas of your life which need to be controlled by God. However, don't wait until Friday to confess these sins; confess any sin you commit immediately. Friday's quiet time will take a longer look at your whole life. Be careful not to document your sins; make abbreviations for difficult sin areas. Plan positive ways to break bad habits and inconsistent behavior. Focus upon the fruit of the Holy Spirit and letting God develop them in your heart.

SATURDAY Petition/Personal Needs
Purpose—to bring your personal needs before God.

How to Begin—before placing any need on this list, ask yourself if it is a selfish desire. Write down each need that is consistent with God's will and the date you begin praying for it. Remember that Jesus said, "You have not because you ask not."

Prayer Diary
Purpose—to give daily regularity to your prayer life, and to record commitments, vows, and spiritual growth.

How to Begin—after using each day's prayer list, check off the box next to the correct date. This will help determine your faithfulness in prayer. The blanks are to be used as a diary to record verbal prayers. God remembers your prayers; the diary will help you remember them too. Try to write something every day. Level with the Lord about your spiritual successes and failures. The more you put into this diary, the greater your rewards will be.

Answered Prayer
Purpose—to develop a thankful heart.

How to Begin—when God positively answers one of your prayers, transfer the request and the answer to this section of your notebook. If you pray faithfully according to the Word, you will soon find you have a long list of answered prayers. Use this list to give glory back to God. Thank Him often for His answers.

1. Tell God how much you love Him:_____
_____
_____
_____
_____

2. Reflect on each of God's attributes. (Check each box as you finish):

☐ God knows everything.   ☐ God is merciful.

☐ God is always present.   ☐ God is truthful.

☐ God has all power.   ☐ God is love.

☐ God is absolutely holy.   ☐ God is eternal.

☐ God is faithful.   ☐ God never changes.

☐ God is completely just.   ☐ God is wisdom.

3. Like the Psalmist, think of creative ways to praise God:_____
_____
_____
_____
_____

4. List the different names of God found in the Bible and consider how each of these names reveals God's character:_____
_____
_____
_____
_____

5. Tell Jesus, the Lamb, how worthy He is. Praise God for giving His great salvation:_____
_____
_____
_____

1. Tell God how much you love Him:_____
   _____
   _____
   _____
   _____

2. Reflect on each of God's attributes. (Check each box as you finish):

   ☐ God knows everything.   ☐ God is merciful.

   ☐ God is always present.   ☐ God is truthful.

   ☐ God has all power.   ☐ God is love.

   ☐ God is absolutely holy.   ☐ God is eternal.

   ☐ God is faithful.   ☐ God never changes.

   ☐ God is completely just.   ☐ God is wisdom.

3. Like the Psalmist, think of creative ways to praise God:_____
   _____
   _____
   _____
   _____

4. List the different names of God found in the Bible and consider how
   each of these names reveals God's character:_____
   _____
   _____
   _____
   _____

5. Tell Jesus, the Lamb, how worthy He is. Praise God for giving His
   great salvation:_____
   _____
   _____
   _____

1. Tell God how much you love Him: _____

_____

_____

_____

2. Reflect on each of God's attributes. (Check each box as you finish):

☐ God knows everything.   ☐ God is merciful.

☐ God is always present.   ☐ God is truthful.

☐ God has all power.   ☐ God is love.

☐ God is absolutely holy.   ☐ God is eternal.

☐ God is faithful.   ☐ God never changes.

☐ God is completely just.   ☐ God is wisdom.

3. Like the Psalmist, think of creative ways to praise God: _____

_____

_____

_____

4. List the different names of God found in the Bible and consider how each of these names reveals God's character: _____

_____

_____

_____

5. Tell Jesus, the Lamb, how worthy He is. Praise God for giving His great salvation: _____

_____

_____

_____

1. Tell God how much you love Him:_____

_____

_____

_____

_____

2. Reflect on each of God's attributes. (Check each box as you finish):

☐ God knows everything.   ☐ God is merciful.

☐ God is always present.   ☐ God is truthful.

☐ God has all power.   ☐ God is love.

☐ God is absolutely holy.   ☐ God is eternal.

☐ God is faithful.   ☐ God never changes.

☐ God is completely just.   ☐ God is wisdom.

3. Like the Psalmist, think of creative ways to praise God:_____

_____

_____

_____

_____

4. List the different names of God found in the Bible and consider how each of these names reveals God's character:_____

_____

_____

_____

5. Tell Jesus, the Lamb, how worthy He is. Praise God for giving His great salvation:_____

_____

_____

_____

1. Tell God how much you love Him:_____

_____

_____

_____

2. Reflect on each of God's attributes. (Check each box as you finish):

☐ God knows everything.   ☐ God is merciful.

☐ God is always present.   ☐ God is truthful.

☐ God has all power.   ☐ God is love.

☐ God is absolutely holy.   ☐ God is eternal.

☐ God is faithful.   ☐ God never changes.

☐ God is completely just.   ☐ God is wisdom.

3. Like the Psalmist, think of creative ways to praise God:_____

_____

_____

_____

_____

4. List the different names of God found in the Bible and consider how each of these names reveals God's character:_____

_____

_____

_____

5. Tell Jesus, the Lamb, how worthy He is. Praise God for giving His great salvation:_____

_____

_____

_____

1. Tell God how much you love Him:_____
_____
_____
_____
_____

2. Reflect on each of God's attributes. (Check each box as you finish):

☐ God knows everything.   ☐ God is merciful.

☐ God is always present.   ☐ God is truthful.

☐ God has all power.   ☐ God is love.

☐ God is absolutely holy.   ☐ God is eternal.

☐ God is faithful.   ☐ God never changes.

☐ God is completely just.   ☐ God is wisdom.

3. Like the Psalmist, think of creative ways to praise God:_____
_____
_____
_____
_____

4. List the different names of God found in the Bible and consider how each of these names reveals God's character:_____
_____
_____
_____
_____

5. Tell Jesus, the Lamb, how worthy He is. Praise God for giving His great salvation:_____
_____
_____
_____

1. Tell God how much you love Him:_____

_____

_____

_____

_____

2. Reflect on each of God's attributes. (Check each box as you finish):

☐ God knows everything.   ☐ God is merciful.

☐ God is always present.   ☐ God is truthful.

☐ God has all power.   ☐ God is love.

☐ God is absolutely holy.   ☐ God is eternal.

☐ God is faithful.   ☐ God never changes.

☐ God is completely just.   ☐ God is wisdom.

3. Like the Psalmist, think of creative ways to praise God:_____

_____

_____

_____

_____

4. List the different names of God found in the Bible and consider how each of these names reveals God's character:_____

_____

_____

_____

_____

5. Tell Jesus, the Lamb, how worthy He is. Praise God for giving His great salvation:_____

_____

_____

_____

1. Tell God how much you love Him:_____
   _____
   _____
   _____
   _____

2. Reflect on each of God's attributes. (Check each box as you finish):

   ☐ God knows everything.   ☐ God is merciful.

   ☐ God is always present.   ☐ God is truthful.

   ☐ God has all power.   ☐ God is love.

   ☐ God is absolutely holy.   ☐ God is eternal.

   ☐ God is faithful.   ☐ God never changes.

   ☐ God is completely just.   ☐ God is wisdom.

3. Like the Psalmist, think of creative ways to praise God:_____
   _____
   _____
   _____
   _____

4. List the different names of God found in the Bible and consider how
   each of these names reveals God's character:_____
   _____
   _____
   _____
   _____

5. Tell Jesus, the Lamb, how worthy He is. Praise God for giving His
   great salvation:_____
   _____
   _____
   _____

1. Tell God how much you love Him:_____
   _____
   _____
   _____
   _____

2. Reflect on each of God's attributes. (Check each box as you finish):

   ☐ God knows everything.   ☐ God is merciful.

   ☐ God is always present.   ☐ God is truthful.

   ☐ God has all power.   ☐ God is love.

   ☐ God is absolutely holy.   ☐ God is eternal.

   ☐ God is faithful.   ☐ God never changes.

   ☐ God is completely just.   ☐ God is wisdom.

3. Like the Psalmist, think of creative ways to praise God:_____
   _____
   _____
   _____
   _____

4. List the different names of God found in the Bible and consider how
   each of these names reveals God's character:_____
   _____
   _____
   _____

5. Tell Jesus, the Lamb, how worthy He is. Praise God for giving His
   great salvation:_____
   _____
   _____
   _____

1. Tell God how much you love Him:_____

_____

_____

_____

2. Reflect on each of God's attributes. (Check each box as you finish):

☐ God knows everything.   ☐ God is merciful.

☐ God is always present.   ☐ God is truthful.

☐ God has all power.   ☐ God is love.

☐ God is absolutely holy.   ☐ God is eternal.

☐ God is faithful.   ☐ God never changes.

☐ God is completely just.   ☐ God is wisdom.

3. Like the Psalmist, think of creative ways to praise God:_____

_____

_____

_____

_____

4. List the different names of God found in the Bible and consider how each of these names reveals God's character:_____

_____

_____

_____

_____

5. Tell Jesus, the Lamb, how worthy He is. Praise God for giving His great salvation:_____

_____

_____

_____

1. Tell God how much you love Him:_____
_____
_____
_____
_____

2. Reflect on each of God's attributes. (Check each box as you finish):

☐ God knows everything.   ☐ God is merciful.

☐ God is always present.   ☐ God is truthful.

☐ God has all power.   ☐ God is love.

☐ God is absolutely holy.   ☐ God is eternal.

☐ God is faithful.   ☐ God never changes.

☐ God is completely just.   ☐ God is wisdom.

3. Like the Psalmist, think of creative ways to praise God:_____
_____
_____
_____
_____

4. List the different names of God found in the Bible and consider how each of these names reveals God's character:_____
_____
_____
_____
_____

5. Tell Jesus, the Lamb, how worthy He is. Praise God for giving His great salvation:_____
_____
_____
_____

1. Tell God how much you love Him:_____
   _____
   _____
   _____
   _____

2. Reflect on each of God's attributes. (Check each box as you finish):

   ☐ God knows everything.   ☐ God is merciful.

   ☐ God is always present.   ☐ God is truthful.

   ☐ God has all power.   ☐ God is love.

   ☐ God is absolutely holy.   ☐ God is eternal.

   ☐ God is faithful.   ☐ God never changes.

   ☐ God is completely just.   ☐ God is wisdom.

3. Like the Psalmist, think of creative ways to praise God:_____
   _____
   _____
   _____
   _____

4. List the different names of God found in the Bible and consider how each of these names reveals God's character:_____
   _____
   _____
   _____
   _____

5. Tell Jesus, the Lamb, how worthy He is. Praise God for giving His great salvation:_____
   _____
   _____
   _____

Name_____Date_____

Prayer steps needed to lead him or her to Christ:

1)_____ ☐ Step Reached

2)_____ ☐ Step Reached

3)_____ ☐ Step Reached

4)_____ ☐ Step Reached

5)_____ ☐ Step Reached

6)_____ ☐ Step Reached

Decision Made_____

Name_____Date_____

Prayer steps needed to lead him or her to Christ:

1)_____ ☐ Step Reached

2)_____ ☐ Step Reached

3)_____ ☐ Step Reached

4)_____ ☐ Step Reached

5)_____ ☐ Step Reached

6)_____ ☐ Step Reached

Decision Made_____

Name_____Date_____

Prayer steps needed to lead him or her to Christ:

1)_____ ☐ Step Reached

2)_____ ☐ Step Reached

3)_____ ☐ Step Reached

4)_____ ☐ Step Reached

5)_____ ☐ Step Reached

6)_____ ☐ Step Reached

Decision Made_____

Monday Intercession/Non-Christians

Name_____Date_____

Prayer steps needed to lead him or her to Christ:

1)_____ ☐ Step Reached

2)_____ ☐ Step Reached

3)_____ ☐ Step Reached

4)_____ ☐ Step Reached

5)_____ ☐ Step Reached

6)_____ ☐ Step Reached

Decision Made_____

Name_____Date_____

Prayer steps needed to lead him or her to Christ:

1)_____ ☐ Step Reached

2)_____ ☐ Step Reached

3)_____ ☐ Step Reached

4)_____ ☐ Step Reached

5)_____ ☐ Step Reached

6)_____ ☐ Step Reached

Decision Made_____

Name_____Date_____

Prayer steps needed to lead him or her to Christ:

1)_____ ☐ Step Reached

2)_____ ☐ Step Reached

3)_____ ☐ Step Reached

4)_____ ☐ Step Reached

5)_____ ☐ Step Reached

6)_____ ☐ Step Reached

Decision Made_____

Name_____Date_____

Prayer steps needed to lead him or her to Christ:

1)_____ ☐ Step Reached
2)_____ ☐ Step Reached
3)_____ ☐ Step Reached
4)_____ ☐ Step Reached
5)_____ ☐ Step Reached
6)_____ ☐ Step Reached

Decision Made_____

Name_____Date_____

Prayer steps needed to lead him or her to Christ:

1)_____ ☐ Step Reached
2)_____ ☐ Step Reached
3)_____ ☐ Step Reached
4)_____ ☐ Step Reached
5)_____ ☐ Step Reached
6)_____ ☐ Step Reached

Decision Made_____

Name_____Date_____

Prayer steps needed to lead him or her to Christ:

1)_____ ☐ Step Reached
2)_____ ☐ Step Reached
3)_____ ☐ Step Reached
4)_____ ☐ Step Reached
5)_____ ☐ Step Reached
6)_____ ☐ Step Reached

Decision Made_____

Name_____ Date_____

Prayer steps needed to lead him or her to Christ:

1)_____ ☐ Step Reached

2)_____ ☐ Step Reached

3)_____ ☐ Step Reached

4)_____ ☐ Step Reached

5)_____ ☐ Step Reached

6)_____ ☐ Step Reached

Decision Made_____

Name_____ Date_____

Prayer steps needed to lead him or her to Christ:

1)_____ ☐ Step Reached

2)_____ ☐ Step Reached

3)_____ ☐ Step Reached

4)_____ ☐ Step Reached

5)_____ ☐ Step Reached

6)_____ ☐ Step Reached

Decision Made_____

Name_____ Date_____

Prayer steps needed to lead him or her to Christ:

1)_____ ☐ Step Reached

2)_____ ☐ Step Reached

3)_____ ☐ Step Reached

4)_____ ☐ Step Reached

5)_____ ☐ Step Reached

6)_____ ☐ Step Reached

Decision Made_____

Name_____ Date_____

Prayer steps needed to lead him or her to Christ:

1)_____ ☐ Step Reached

2)_____ ☐ Step Reached

3)_____ ☐ Step Reached

4)_____ ☐ Step Reached

5)_____ ☐ Step Reached

6)_____ ☐ Step Reached

Decision Made_____

Name_____ Date_____

Prayer steps needed to lead him or her to Christ:

1)_____ ☐ Step Reached

2)_____ ☐ Step Reached

3)_____ ☐ Step Reached

4)_____ ☐ Step Reached

5)_____ ☐ Step Reached

6)_____ ☐ Step Reached

Decision Made_____

Name_____ Date_____

Prayer steps needed to lead him or her to Christ:

1)_____ ☐ Step Reached

2)_____ ☐ Step Reached

3)_____ ☐ Step Reached

4)_____ ☐ Step Reached

5)_____ ☐ Step Reached

6)_____ ☐ Step Reached

Decision Made_____

Name_____Date_____

Prayer steps needed to lead him or her to Christ:

1)_____ ☐ Step Reached

2)_____ ☐ Step Reached

3)_____ ☐ Step Reached

4)_____ ☐ Step Reached

5)_____ ☐ Step Reached

6)_____ ☐ Step Reached

Decision Made_____

Name_____Date_____

Prayer steps needed to lead him or her to Christ:

1)_____ ☐ Step Reached

2)_____ ☐ Step Reached

3)_____ ☐ Step Reached

4)_____ ☐ Step Reached

5)_____ ☐ Step Reached

6)_____ ☐ Step Reached

Decision Made_____

Name_____Date_____

Prayer steps needed to lead him or her to Christ:

1)_____ ☐ Step Reached

2)_____ ☐ Step Reached

3)_____ ☐ Step Reached

4)_____ ☐ Step Reached

5)_____ ☐ Step Reached

6)_____ ☐ Step Reached

Decision Made_____

Name_____Date_____

Prayer steps needed to lead him or her to Christ:

1)_____ ☐ Step Reached

2)_____ ☐ Step Reached

3)_____ ☐ Step Reached

4)_____ ☐ Step Reached

5)_____ ☐ Step Reached

6)_____ ☐ Step Reached

Decision Made_____

Name_____Date_____

Prayer steps needed to lead him or her to Christ:

1)_____ ☐ Step Reached

2)_____ ☐ Step Reached

3)_____ ☐ Step Reached

4)_____ ☐ Step Reached

5)_____ ☐ Step Reached

6)_____ ☐ Step Reached

Decision Made_____

Name_____Date_____

Prayer steps needed to lead him or her to Christ:

1)_____ ☐ Step Reached

2)_____ ☐ Step Reached

3)_____ ☐ Step Reached

4)_____ ☐ Step Reached

5)_____ ☐ Step Reached

6)_____ ☐ Step Reached

Decision Made_____

Name_____ Date_____

Prayer steps needed to lead him or her to Christ:

1)_____ ☐ Step Reached

2)_____ ☐ Step Reached

3)_____ ☐ Step Reached

4)_____ ☐ Step Reached

5)_____ ☐ Step Reached

6)_____ ☐ Step Reached

Decision Made_____

Name_____ Date_____

Prayer steps needed to lead him or her to Christ:

1)_____ ☐ Step Reached

2)_____ ☐ Step Reached

3)_____ ☐ Step Reached

4)_____ ☐ Step Reached

5)_____ ☐ Step Reached

6)_____ ☐ Step Reached

Decision Made_____

Name_____ Date_____

Prayer steps needed to lead him or her to Christ:

1)_____ ☐ Step Reached

2)_____ ☐ Step Reached

3)_____ ☐ Step Reached

4)_____ ☐ Step Reached

5)_____ ☐ Step Reached

6)_____ ☐ Step Reached

Decision Made_____

Name_____Date_____

Prayer steps needed to lead him or her to Christ:

1)_____ ☐ Step Reached

2)_____ ☐ Step Reached

3)_____ ☐ Step Reached

4)_____ ☐ Step Reached

5)_____ ☐ Step Reached

6)_____ ☐ Step Reached

Decision Made_____

Name_____Date_____

Prayer steps needed to lead him or her to Christ:

1)_____ ☐ Step Reached

2)_____ ☐ Step Reached

3)_____ ☐ Step Reached

4)_____ ☐ Step Reached

5)_____ ☐ Step Reached

6)_____ ☐ Step Reached

Decision Made_____

Name_____Date_____

Prayer steps needed to lead him or her to Christ:

1)_____ ☐ Step Reached

2)_____ ☐ Step Reached

3)_____ ☐ Step Reached

4)_____ ☐ Step Reached

5)_____ ☐ Step Reached

6)_____ ☐ Step Reached

Decision Made_____

Name_____Date_____

Prayer steps needed to lead him or her to Christ:

1)_____ ☐ Step Reached

2)_____ ☐ Step Reached

3)_____ ☐ Step Reached

4)_____ ☐ Step Reached

5)_____ ☐ Step Reached

6)_____ ☐ Step Reached

Decision Made_____

Name_____Date_____

Prayer steps needed to lead him or her to Christ:

1)_____ ☐ Step Reached

2)_____ ☐ Step Reached

3)_____ ☐ Step Reached

4)_____ ☐ Step Reached

5)_____ ☐ Step Reached

6)_____ ☐ Step Reached

Decision Made_____

Name_____Date_____

Prayer steps needed to lead him or her to Christ:

1)_____ ☐ Step Reached

2)_____ ☐ Step Reached

3)_____ ☐ Step Reached

4)_____ ☐ Step Reached

5)_____ ☐ Step Reached

6)_____ ☐ Step Reached

Decision Made_____

Name_____ Date_____

Prayer steps needed to lead him or her to Christ:

1)_____ ☐ Step Reached
2)_____ ☐ Step Reached
3)_____ ☐ Step Reached
4)_____ ☐ Step Reached
5)_____ ☐ Step Reached
6)_____ ☐ Step Reached

Decision Made_____

Name_____ Date_____

Prayer steps needed to lead him or her to Christ:

1)_____ ☐ Step Reached
2)_____ ☐ Step Reached
3)_____ ☐ Step Reached
4)_____ ☐ Step Reached
5)_____ ☐ Step Reached
6)_____ ☐ Step Reached

Decision Made_____

Name_____ Date_____

Prayer steps needed to lead him or her to Christ:

1)_____ ☐ Step Reached
2)_____ ☐ Step Reached
3)_____ ☐ Step Reached
4)_____ ☐ Step Reached
5)_____ ☐ Step Reached
6)_____ ☐ Step Reached

Decision Made_____

Name_____Date_____

Prayer steps needed to lead him or her to Christ:

1)_____ ☐ Step Reached

2)_____ ☐ Step Reached

3)_____ ☐ Step Reached

4)_____ ☐ Step Reached

5)_____ ☐ Step Reached

6)_____ ☐ Step Reached

Decision Made_____

Name_____Date_____

Prayer steps needed to lead him or her to Christ:

1)_____ ☐ Step Reached

2)_____ ☐ Step Reached

3)_____ ☐ Step Reached

4)_____ ☐ Step Reached

5)_____ ☐ Step Reached

6)_____ ☐ Step Reached

Decision Made_____

Name_____Date_____

Prayer steps needed to lead him or her to Christ:

1)_____ ☐ Step Reached

2)_____ ☐ Step Reached

3)_____ ☐ Step Reached

4)_____ ☐ Step Reached

5)_____ ☐ Step Reached

6)_____ ☐ Step Reached

Decision Made_____

Tuesday Thanksgiving

1. Thank the Lord for answered prayer (look at ANSWERED PRAYER in the back of this notebook).

2. Thank the Lord for good health, material blessings, and life in general. List specific things:_____
    _____
    _____
    _____

3. Thank the Lord for spiritual blessings:_____
    _____
    _____
    _____

4. Thank the Lord for all persecution and misfortune:_____
    _____
    _____
    _____

5. Thank the Lord for future blessings. List things for which you will give thanks (in faith) before they happen:_____
    _____
    _____
    _____

6. Thank the Lord for your Christian friends:_____
    _____
    _____
    _____

7. Thank the Lord for His death on the cross and what it means:
    _____
    _____
    _____
    _____

Tuesday   Thanksgiving

1. Thank the Lord for answered prayer (look at ANSWERED PRAYER in the back of this notebook).

2. Thank the Lord for good health, material blessings, and life in general. List specific things:_____
   _____
   _____
   _____

3. Thank the Lord for spiritual blessings:_____
   _____
   _____
   _____

4. Thank the Lord for all persecution and misfortune:_____
   _____
   _____
   _____

5. Thank the Lord for future blessings. List things for which you will give thanks (in faith) before they happen:_____
   _____
   _____
   _____

6. Thank the Lord for your Christian friends:_____
   _____
   _____
   _____

7. Thank the Lord for His death on the cross and what it means:
   _____
   _____
   _____
   _____

Tuesday   Thanksgiving

1. Thank the Lord for answered prayer (look at ANSWERED PRAYER in the back of this notebook).

2. Thank the Lord for good health, material blessings, and life in general. List specific things:_____

_____

_____

_____

3. Thank the Lord for spiritual blessings:_____

_____

_____

_____

4. Thank the Lord for all persecution and misfortune:_____

_____

_____

_____

5. Thank the Lord for future blessings. List things for which you will give thanks (in faith) before they happen:_____

_____

_____

_____

6. Thank the Lord for your Christian friends:_____

_____

_____

_____

7. Thank the Lord for His death on the cross and what it means:

_____

_____

_____

_____

Tuesday   Thanksgiving

1. Thank the Lord for answered prayer (look at ANSWERED PRAYER in the back of this notebook).

2. Thank the Lord for good health, material blessings, and life in general. List specific things:_____
_____
_____
_____

3. Thank the Lord for spiritual blessings:_____
_____
_____
_____

4. Thank the Lord for all persecution and misfortune:_____
_____
_____
_____

5. Thank the Lord for future blessings. List things for which you will give thanks (in faith) before they happen:_____
_____
_____
_____

6. Thank the Lord for your Christian friends:_____
_____
_____
_____

7. Thank the Lord for His death on the cross and what it means:
_____
_____
_____
_____

Tuesday   Thanksgiving

1. Thank the Lord for answered prayer (look at ANSWERED PRAYER in the back of this notebook).

2. Thank the Lord for good health, material blessings, and life in general. List specific things:_____
   _____
   _____
   _____

3. Thank the Lord for spiritual blessings:_____
   _____
   _____
   _____

4. Thank the Lord for all persecution and misfortune:_____
   _____
   _____
   _____

5. Thank the Lord for future blessings. List things for which you will give thanks (in faith) before they happen:_____
   _____
   _____
   _____

6. Thank the Lord for your Christian friends:_____
   _____
   _____
   _____

7. Thank the Lord for His death on the cross and what it means:
   _____
   _____
   _____
   _____

1. Thank the Lord for answered prayer (look at ANSWERED PRAYER in the back of this notebook).

2. Thank the Lord for good health, material blessings, and life in general. List specific things:_____
_____
_____
_____

3. Thank the Lord for spiritual blessings:_____
_____
_____
_____

4. Thank the Lord for all persecution and misfortune:_____
_____
_____
_____

5. Thank the Lord for future blessings. List things for which you will give thanks (in faith) before they happen:_____
_____
_____
_____

6. Thank the Lord for your Christian friends:_____
_____
_____
_____

7. Thank the Lord for His death on the cross and what it means:
_____
_____
_____
_____

1. Thank the Lord for answered prayer (look at ANSWERED PRAYER in the back of this notebook).

2. Thank the Lord for good health, material blessings, and life in general. List specific things:_____
   _____
   _____
   _____

3. Thank the Lord for spiritual blessings:_____
   _____
   _____
   _____

4. Thank the Lord for all persecution and misfortune:_____
   _____
   _____
   _____

5. Thank the Lord for future blessings. List things for which you will give thanks (in faith) before they happen:_____
   _____
   _____
   _____

6. Thank the Lord for your Christian friends:_____
   _____
   _____
   _____

7. Thank the Lord for His death on the cross and what it means:
   _____
   _____
   _____
   _____

Tuesday　　Thanksgiving

1. Thank the Lord for answered prayer (look at ANSWERED PRAYER in the back of this notebook).

2. Thank the Lord for good health, material blessings, and life in general. List specific things:_____
_____
_____
_____

3. Thank the Lord for spiritual blessings:_____
_____
_____
_____

4. Thank the Lord for all persecution and misfortune:_____
_____
_____
_____

5. Thank the Lord for future blessings. List things for which you will give thanks (in faith) before they happen:_____
_____
_____
_____

6. Thank the Lord for your Christian friends:_____
_____
_____
_____

7. Thank the Lord for His death on the cross and what it means:
_____
_____
_____
_____

Tuesday — Thanksgiving

1. Thank the Lord for answered prayer (look at ANSWERED PRAYER in the back of this notebook).

2. Thank the Lord for good health, material blessings, and life in general. List specific things:_____

_____

_____

_____

3. Thank the Lord for spiritual blessings:_____

_____

_____

_____

4. Thank the Lord for all persecution and misfortune:_____

_____

_____

_____

5. Thank the Lord for future blessings. List things for which you will give thanks (in faith) before they happen:_____

_____

_____

_____

6. Thank the Lord for your Christian friends:_____

_____

_____

_____

7. Thank the Lord for His death on the cross and what it means:

_____

_____

_____

_____

Tuesday — Thanksgiving

1. Thank the Lord for answered prayer (look at ANSWERED PRAYER in the back of this notebook).

2. Thank the Lord for good health, material blessings, and life in general. List specific things:_____
   _____
   _____
   _____

3. Thank the Lord for spiritual blessings:_____
   _____
   _____
   _____

4. Thank the Lord for all persecution and misfortune:_____
   _____
   _____
   _____

5. Thank the Lord for future blessings. List things for which you will give thanks (in faith) before they happen:_____
   _____
   _____
   _____

6. Thank the Lord for your Christian friends:_____
   _____
   _____
   _____

7. Thank the Lord for His death on the cross and what it means:
   _____
   _____
   _____
   _____

1. Thank the Lord for answered prayer (look at ANSWERED PRAYER in the back of this notebook).

2. Thank the Lord for good health, material blessings, and life in general. List specific things:_____
   _____
   _____
   _____

3. Thank the Lord for spiritual blessings:_____
   _____
   _____
   _____

4. Thank the Lord for all persecution and misfortune:_____
   _____
   _____
   _____

5. Thank the Lord for future blessings. List things for which you will give thanks (in faith) before they happen:_____
   _____
   _____
   _____

6. Thank the Lord for your Christian friends:_____
   _____
   _____
   _____

7. Thank the Lord for His death on the cross and what it means:
   _____
   _____
   _____
   _____

Tuesday   Thanksgiving

1. Thank the Lord for answered prayer (look at ANSWERED PRAYER in the back of this notebook).

2. Thank the Lord for good health, material blessings, and life in general. List specific things:_____
_____
_____
_____

3. Thank the Lord for spiritual blessings:_____
_____
_____
_____

4. Thank the Lord for all persecution and misfortune:_____
_____
_____
_____

5. Thank the Lord for future blessings. List things for which you will give thanks (in faith) before they happen:_____
_____
_____
_____

6. Thank the Lord for your Christian friends:_____
_____
_____
_____

7. Thank the Lord for His death on the cross and what it means:
_____
_____
_____
_____

Wednesday Intercession/Missions

Missionary's Name_____ Birthday_____

Wife's Name_____ Birthday_____

Child's Name_____ Birthday_____

Child's Name_____ Birthday_____

Child's Name_____ Birthday_____

Child's Name_____ Birthday_____

NEEDS   DATES

_____

_____

_____

_____

_____

_____

_____

ANSWERS   DATES

_____

_____

_____

_____

_____

_____

_____

Field Address_____

_____

_____

Home Address_____

_____

_____

Times Written_____

Missionary's Name _____ Birthday _____

Wife's Name _____ Birthday _____

Child's Name _____ Birthday _____

Child's Name _____ Birthday _____

Child's Name _____ Birthday _____

Child's Name _____ Birthday _____

NEEDS   DATES

_____

_____

_____

_____

_____

_____

_____

ANSWERS   DATES

_____

_____

_____

_____

_____

_____

Field Address _____

_____

Home Address _____

_____

Times Written _____

Wednesday Intercession/Missions

Missionary's Name_____ Birthday_____

Wife's Name_____ Birthday_____

Child's Name_____ Birthday_____

Child's Name_____ Birthday_____

Child's Name_____ Birthday_____

Child's Name_____ Birthday_____

NEEDS	DATES

_____

_____

_____

_____

_____

_____

_____

ANSWERS	DATES

_____

_____

_____

_____

_____

_____

_____

Field Address_____

_____

_____

Home Address_____

_____

_____

Times Written_____

Wednesday   Intercession/Missions

Missionary's Name_____Birthday_____

Wife's Name_____Birthday_____

Child's Name_____Birthday_____

Child's Name_____Birthday_____

Child's Name_____Birthday_____

Child's Name_____Birthday_____

NEEDS   DATES

_____

_____

_____

_____

_____

_____

ANSWERS   DATES

_____

_____

_____

_____

_____

_____

Field Address_____

_____

Home Address_____

_____

_____

Times Written_____

Wednesday Intercession/Missions

Missionary's Name_____Birthday_____

Wife's Name_____Birthday_____

Child's Name_____Birthday_____

Child's Name_____Birthday_____

Child's Name_____Birthday_____

Child's Name_____Birthday_____

NEEDS   DATES

_____

_____

_____

_____

_____

_____

_____

ANSWERS   DATES

_____

_____

_____

_____

_____

_____

Field Address_____

_____

_____

Home Address_____

_____

_____

Times Written_____

Wednesday Intercession/Missions

Missionary's Name_____ Birthday_____

Wife's Name_____ Birthday_____

Child's Name_____ Birthday_____

Child's Name_____ Birthday_____

Child's Name_____ Birthday_____

Child's Name_____ Birthday_____

NEEDS	DATES

ANSWERS	DATES

Field Address_____

_____

_____

Home Address_____

_____

_____

Times Written_____

Wednesday Intercession/Missions

Missionary's Name_____ Birthday_____

Wife's Name_____ Birthday_____

Child's Name_____ Birthday_____

Child's Name_____ Birthday_____

Child's Name_____ Birthday_____

Child's Name_____ Birthday_____

NEEDS	DATES

ANSWERS	DATES

Field Address_____

Home Address_____

Times Written_____

Wednesday Intercession/Missions

Missionary's Name_____ Birthday_____

Wife's Name_____ Birthday_____

Child's Name_____ Birthday_____

Child's Name_____ Birthday_____

Child's Name_____ Birthday_____

Child's Name_____ Birthday_____

NEEDS	DATES

ANSWERS ... DATES

Field Address_____

Home Address_____

Times Written_____

Wednesday Intercession/Missions

Missionary's Name_____Birthday_____

Wife's Name_____Birthday_____

Child's Name_____Birthday_____

Child's Name_____Birthday_____

Child's Name_____Birthday_____

Child's Name_____Birthday_____

NEEDS	DATES
_____	_____
_____	_____
_____	_____
_____	_____
_____	_____
_____	_____

ANSWERS	DATES
_____	_____
_____	_____
_____	_____
_____	_____
_____	_____

Field Address_____

_____

Home Address_____

_____

Times Written_____

Wednesday Intercession/Missions

Missionary's Name _____ Birthday _____

Wife's Name _____ Birthday _____

Child's Name _____ Birthday _____

Child's Name _____ Birthday _____

Child's Name _____ Birthday _____

Child's Name _____ Birthday _____

NEEDS	DATES
_____	_____
_____	_____
_____	_____
_____	_____
_____	_____
_____	_____
_____	_____

ANSWERS	DATES
_____	_____
_____	_____
_____	_____
_____	_____
_____	_____
_____	_____
_____	_____

Field Address _____

_____

Home Address _____

_____

Times Written _____

Wednesday Intercession/Missions

Missionary's Name_____ Birthday_____

Wife's Name_____ Birthday_____

Child's Name_____ Birthday_____

Child's Name_____ Birthday_____

Child's Name_____ Birthday_____

Child's Name_____ Birthday_____

NEEDS   DATES

_____

_____

_____

_____

_____

_____

ANSWERS   DATES

_____

_____

_____

_____

_____

_____

_____

Field Address_____

_____

Home Address_____

_____

_____

Times Written_____

Missionary's Name_____ Birthday_____

Wife's Name_____ Birthday_____

Child's Name_____ Birthday_____

Child's Name_____ Birthday_____

Child's Name_____ Birthday_____

Child's Name_____ Birthday_____

NEEDS	DATES

ANSWERS	DATES

Field Address_____

_____

Home Address_____

_____

Times Written_____

Thursday Intercession/Christians

Name_____ Date_____

Needs_____

_____

_____

Answers_____

_____

_____

Name_____

Needs_____

_____

Answers_____

_____

Name_____

Needs_____

_____

Answers_____

_____

_____

Name_____

Needs_____

_____

Answers_____

_____

_____

Thursday Intercession/Christians

Name_____ Date_____

Needs_____

_____

_____

Answers_____

_____

_____

Name_____

Needs_____

_____

Answers_____

_____

_____

Name_____

Needs_____

_____

_____

Answers_____

_____

_____

Name_____

Needs_____

_____

_____

Answers_____

_____

_____

Name_____ Date_____

Needs_____

_____

_____

Answers_____

_____

_____

_____

Name_____

Needs_____

_____

Answers_____

_____

_____

Name_____

Needs_____

_____

_____

Answers_____

_____

_____

_____

Name_____

Needs_____

_____

_____

Answers_____

_____

_____

_____

Thursday Intercession/Christians

Name _____ Date _____

Needs _____

_____

_____

Answers _____

_____

_____

Name _____

Needs _____

_____

Answers _____

_____

Name _____

Needs _____

_____

_____

Answers _____

_____

_____

Name _____

Needs _____

_____

Answers _____

_____

_____

Thursday Intercession/Christians

Name_____ Date_____
Needs_____
_____
_____
Answers_____
_____
_____

Name_____
Needs_____
_____
Answers_____
_____

Name_____
Needs_____
_____
_____
Answers_____
_____
_____

Name_____
Needs_____
_____
_____
Answers_____
_____
_____

Thursday Intercession/Christians

Name_____ Date_____

Needs_____

_____

_____

Answers_____

_____

_____

Name_____

Needs_____

_____

Answers_____

_____

Name_____

Needs_____

_____

Answers_____

_____

_____

Name_____

Needs_____

_____

_____

Answers_____

_____

_____

Thursday Intercession/Christians

Name_____ Date_____

Needs_____
_____
_____

Answers_____
_____
_____

Name_____

Needs_____
_____

Answers_____
_____

Name_____

Needs_____
_____

Answers_____
_____
_____

Name_____

Needs_____
_____

Answers_____
_____
_____

Thursday Intercession/Christians

Name_____ Date_____
Needs_____
_____
_____
Answers_____
_____
_____

Name_____
Needs_____
_____
Answers_____
_____

Name_____
Needs_____
_____
_____
Answers_____
_____
_____

Name_____
Needs_____
_____
_____
Answers_____
_____
_____

Name_____ Date_____

Needs_____

_____

_____

Answers_____

_____

_____

Name_____

Needs_____

_____

Answers_____

_____

Name_____

Needs_____

_____

_____

Answers_____

_____

_____

Name_____

Needs_____

_____

_____

Answers_____

_____

_____

Thursday Intercession/Christians

Name_____ Date_____

Needs_____
_____
_____

Answers_____
_____
_____

Name_____

Needs_____
_____

Answers_____
_____

Name_____

Needs_____
_____
_____

Answers_____
_____
_____

Name_____

Needs_____
_____
_____

Answers_____
_____
_____

Name_____ Date_____

Needs_____
_____
_____

Answers_____
_____
_____

Name_____

Needs_____
_____

Answers_____
_____

Name_____

Needs_____
_____
_____

Answers_____
_____
_____

Name_____

Needs_____
_____
_____

Answers_____
_____
_____

Thursday Intercession/Christians

Name_____ Date_____
Needs_____
_____
_____
Answers_____
_____
_____

Name_____
Needs_____
_____
Answers_____
_____

Name_____
Needs_____
_____
_____
Answers_____
_____
_____

Name_____
Needs_____
_____
_____
Answers_____
_____
_____

Friday   Personal Confession

1. Spiritual areas of my life that are not right and must be confessed:

_____

_____

_____

_____

2. Physical areas of my life that are not right and must be confessed:

_____

_____

_____

_____

3. Problems at work (or school):_____

_____

_____

_____

4. Problems with my attitudes:_____

_____

_____

_____

5. Reflect upon the fruit of the Spirit. How can I develop each character
   quality more fully:

☐ Love_____

☐ Joy_____

☐ Peace_____

☐ Patience_____

☐ Kindness_____

☐ Goodness_____

☐ Faithfulness_____

☐ Gentleness_____

☐ Self-control_____

Friday — Personal Confession

1. Spiritual areas of my life that are not right and must be confessed:

_____

_____

_____

_____

2. Physical areas of my life that are not right and must be confessed:

_____

_____

_____

_____

3. Problems at work (or school):_____

_____

_____

_____

4. Problems with my attitudes:_____

_____

_____

_____

5. Reflect upon the fruit of the Spirit. How can I develop each character quality more fully:

☐ Love_____

☐ Joy_____

☐ Peace_____

☐ Patience_____

☐ Kindness_____

☐ Goodness_____

☐ Faithfulness_____

☐ Gentleness_____

☐ Self-control_____

Friday Personal Confession

1. Spiritual areas of my life that are not right and must be confessed:
   _____
   _____
   _____
   _____

2. Physical areas of my life that are not right and must be confessed:
   _____
   _____
   _____
   _____

3. Problems at work (or school):_____
   _____
   _____
   _____

4. Problems with my attitudes:_____
   _____
   _____
   _____

5. Reflect upon the fruit of the Spirit. How can I develop each character quality more fully:

   ☐ Love_____
   ☐ Joy_____
   ☐ Peace_____
   ☐ Patience_____
   ☐ Kindness_____
   ☐ Goodness_____
   ☐ Faithfulness_____
   ☐ Gentleness_____
   ☐ Self-control_____

Friday   Personal Confession

1. Spiritual areas of my life that are not right and must be confessed:

_____

_____

_____

_____

2. Physical areas of my life that are not right and must be confessed:

_____

_____

_____

_____

3. Problems at work (or school):_____

_____

_____

_____

4. Problems with my attitudes:_____

_____

_____

_____

5. Reflect upon the fruit of the Spirit. How can I develop each character quality more fully:

☐ Love_____

☐ Joy_____

☐ Peace_____

☐ Patience_____

☐ Kindness_____

☐ Goodness_____

☐ Faithfulness_____

☐ Gentleness_____

☐ Self-control_____

Friday   Personal Confession

1. Spiritual areas of my life that are not right and must be confessed:

_____

_____

_____

_____

2. Physical areas of my life that are not right and must be confessed:

_____

_____

_____

_____

3. Problems at work (or school):_____

_____

_____

_____

4. Problems with my attitudes:_____

_____

_____

_____

5. Reflect upon the fruit of the Spirit. How can I develop each character quality more fully:

☐ Love_____

☐ Joy_____

☐ Peace_____

☐ Patience_____

☐ Kindness_____

☐ Goodness_____

☐ Faithfulness_____

☐ Gentleness_____

☐ Self-control_____

Friday — Personal Confession

1. Spiritual areas of my life that are not right and must be confessed:

   _____
   _____
   _____
   _____

2. Physical areas of my life that are not right and must be confessed:

   _____
   _____
   _____
   _____

3. Problems at work (or school):_____

   _____
   _____
   _____

4. Problems with my attitudes:_____

   _____
   _____
   _____

5. Reflect upon the fruit of the Spirit. How can I develop each character quality more fully:

   ☐ Love_____
   ☐ Joy_____
   ☐ Peace_____
   ☐ Patience_____
   ☐ Kindness_____
   ☐ Goodness_____
   ☐ Faithfulness_____
   ☐ Gentleness_____
   ☐ Self-control_____

Friday Personal Confession

1. Spiritual areas of my life that are not right and must be confessed:

_____

_____

_____

_____

2. Physical areas of my life that are not right and must be confessed:

_____

_____

_____

_____

3. Problems at work (or school):_____

_____

_____

_____

4. Problems with my attitudes:_____

_____

_____

_____

5. Reflect upon the fruit of the Spirit. How can I develop each character quality more fully:

☐ Love_____

☐ Joy_____

☐ Peace_____

☐ Patience_____

☐ Kindness_____

☐ Goodness_____

☐ Faithfulness_____

☐ Gentleness_____

☐ Self-control_____

Friday — Personal Confession

1. Spiritual areas of my life that are not right and must be confessed:

_____

_____

_____

_____

2. Physical areas of my life that are not right and must be confessed:

_____

_____

_____

_____

3. Problems at work (or school): _____

_____

_____

_____

4. Problems with my attitudes: _____

_____

_____

_____

5. Reflect upon the fruit of the Spirit. How can I develop each character quality more fully:

☐ Love _____

☐ Joy _____

☐ Peace _____

☐ Patience _____

☐ Kindness _____

☐ Goodness _____

☐ Faithfulness _____

☐ Gentleness _____

☐ Self-control _____

1. Spiritual areas of my life that are not right and must be confessed:

_____

_____

_____

_____

2. Physical areas of my life that are not right and must be confessed:

_____

_____

_____

_____

3. Problems at work (or school):_____

_____

_____

_____

4. Problems with my attitudes:_____

_____

_____

_____

5. Reflect upon the fruit of the Spirit. How can I develop each character quality more fully:

☐ Love_____

☐ Joy_____

☐ Peace_____

☐ Patience_____

☐ Kindness_____

☐ Goodness_____

☐ Faithfulness_____

☐ Gentleness_____

☐ Self-control_____

1. Spiritual areas of my life that are not right and must be confessed:

_____
_____
_____
_____

2. Physical areas of my life that are not right and must be confessed:

_____
_____
_____
_____

3. Problems at work (or school):_____
_____
_____
_____

4. Problems with my attitudes:_____
_____
_____
_____

5. Reflect upon the fruit of the Spirit. How can I develop each character quality more fully:

☐ Love_____
☐ Joy_____
☐ Peace_____
☐ Patience_____
☐ Kindness_____
☐ Goodness_____
☐ Faithfulness_____
☐ Gentleness_____
☐ Self-control_____

1. Spiritual areas of my life that are not right and must be confessed:

_____

_____

_____

_____

2. Physical areas of my life that are not right and must be confessed:

_____

_____

_____

_____

3. Problems at work (or school):_____

_____

_____

_____

4. Problems with my attitudes:_____

_____

_____

_____

5. Reflect upon the fruit of the Spirit. How can I develop each character quality more fully:

☐ Love_____

☐ Joy_____

☐ Peace_____

☐ Patience_____

☐ Kindness_____

☐ Goodness_____

☐ Faithfulness_____

☐ Gentleness_____

☐ Self-control_____

Friday   Personal Confession

1. Spiritual areas of my life that are not right and must be confessed:

_____

_____

_____

_____

2. Physical areas of my life that are not right and must be confessed:

_____

_____

_____

_____

3. Problems at work (or school):_____

_____

_____

_____

4. Problems with my attitudes:_____

_____

_____

_____

5. Reflect upon the fruit of the Spirit. How can I develop each character quality more fully:

☐ Love_____

☐ Joy_____

☐ Peace_____

☐ Patience_____

☐ Kindness_____

☐ Goodness_____

☐ Faithfulness_____

☐ Gentleness_____

☐ Self-control_____

Saturday   Petition/Personal Needs

Personal Need_____
_____Date_____

Answer_____
_____Date_____

Personal Need_____
_____Date_____

Answer_____
_____Date_____

Personal Need_____
_____Date_____

Answer_____
_____Date_____

Personal Need_____
_____Date_____

Answer_____
_____Date_____

Personal Need_____
_____Date_____

Answer_____
_____Date_____

Personal Need_____
_____Date_____

Answer_____
_____Date_____

Saturday — Petition/Personal Needs

Personal Need_____
_____Date_____
Answer_____
_____Date_____

Personal Need_____
_____Date_____
Answer_____
_____Date_____

Personal Need_____
_____Date_____
Answer_____
_____Date_____

Personal Need_____
_____Date_____
Answer_____
_____Date_____

Personal Need_____
_____Date_____
Answer_____
_____Date_____

Personal Need_____
_____Date_____
Answer_____
_____Date_____

Saturday   Petition/Personal Needs

Personal Need_____
_____Date_____

Answer_____
_____Date_____

Personal Need_____
_____Date_____

Answer_____
_____Date_____

Personal Need_____
_____Date_____

Answer_____
_____Date_____

Personal Need_____
_____Date_____

Answer_____
_____Date_____

Personal Need_____
_____Date_____

Answer_____
_____Date_____

Personal Need_____
_____Date_____

Answer_____
_____Date_____

Saturday Petition/Personal Needs

Personal Need_____

_____Date_____

Answer_____

_____Date_____

Personal Need_____

_____Date_____

Answer_____

_____Date_____

Personal Need_____

_____Date_____

Answer_____

_____Date_____

Personal Need_____

_____Date_____

Answer_____

_____Date_____

Personal Need_____

_____Date_____

Answer_____

_____Date_____

Personal Need_____

_____Date_____

Answer_____

_____Date_____

Saturday Petition/Personal Needs

Personal Need_____
_____Date_____

Answer_____
_____Date_____

Personal Need_____
_____Date_____

Answer_____
_____Date_____

Personal Need_____
_____Date_____

Answer_____
_____Date_____

Personal Need_____
_____Date_____

Answer_____
_____Date_____

Personal Need_____
_____Date_____

Answer_____
_____Date_____

Personal Need_____
_____Date_____

Answer_____
_____Date_____

Saturday Petition/Personal Needs

Personal Need_____

_____Date_____

Answer_____

_____Date_____

Personal Need_____

_____Date_____

Answer_____

_____Date_____

Personal Need_____

_____Date_____

Answer_____

_____Date_____

Personal Need_____

_____Date_____

Answer_____

_____Date_____

Personal Need_____

_____Date_____

Answer_____

_____Date_____

Personal Need_____

_____Date_____

Answer_____

_____Date_____

Saturday   Petition/Personal Needs

Personal Need_____
_____Date_____

Answer_____
_____Date_____

Personal Need_____
_____Date_____

Answer_____
_____Date_____

Personal Need_____
_____Date_____

Answer_____
_____Date_____

Personal Need_____
_____Date_____

Answer_____
_____Date_____

Personal Need_____
_____Date_____

Answer_____
_____Date_____

Personal Need_____
_____Date_____

Answer_____
_____Date_____

Saturday Petition/Personal Needs

Personal Need_____
_____Date_____

Answer_____
_____Date_____

Personal Need_____
_____Date_____

Answer_____
_____Date_____

Personal Need_____
_____Date_____

Answer_____
_____Date_____

Personal Need_____
_____Date_____

Answer_____
_____Date_____

Personal Need_____
_____Date_____

Answer_____
_____Date_____

Personal Need_____
_____Date_____

Answer_____
_____Date_____

Personal Need_____
_____Date_____

Answer_____
_____Date_____

Personal Need_____
_____Date_____

Answer_____
_____Date_____

Personal Need_____
_____Date_____

Answer_____
_____Date_____

Personal Need_____
_____Date_____

Answer_____
_____Date_____

Personal Need_____
_____Date_____

Answer_____
_____Date_____

Personal Need_____
_____Date_____

Answer_____
_____Date_____

Personal Need_____

_____Date_____

Answer_____

_____Date_____

Personal Need_____

_____Date_____

Answer_____

_____Date_____

Personal Need_____

_____Date_____

Answer_____

_____Date_____

Personal Need_____

_____Date_____

Answer_____

_____Date_____

Personal Need_____

_____Date_____

Answer_____

_____Date_____

Personal Need_____

_____Date_____

Answer_____

_____Date_____

Saturday Petition/Personal Needs

Personal Need_____
_____Date_____
Answer_____
_____Date_____

Personal Need_____
_____Date_____
Answer_____
_____Date_____

Personal Need_____
_____Date_____
Answer_____
_____Date_____

Personal Need_____
_____Date_____
Answer_____
_____Date_____

Personal Need_____
_____Date_____
Answer_____
_____Date_____

Personal Need_____
_____Date_____
Answer_____
_____Date_____

Saturday — Petition/Personal Needs

Personal Need_____

_____Date_____

Answer_____

_____Date_____

Personal Need_____

_____Date_____

Answer_____

_____Date_____

Personal Need_____

_____Date_____

Answer_____

_____Date_____

Personal Need_____

_____Date_____

Answer_____

_____Date_____

Personal Need_____

_____Date_____

Answer_____

_____Date_____

Personal Need_____

_____Date_____

Answer_____

_____Date_____

Prayer Diary

☐17._____
_____
_____

☐18._____
_____
_____

☐19._____
_____
_____

☐20._____
_____
_____

☐21._____
_____
_____

☐22._____
_____
_____

☐23._____
_____
_____

☐24._____
_____
_____

☐25._____
_____
_____

Prayer Diary

☐26._____

_____

_____

☐27._____

_____

_____

☐28._____

_____

_____

☐29._____

_____

_____

☐30._____

_____

_____

☐31._____

_____

_____

Prayer Diary

"Pray without ceasing."

—1 Thess. 5:17

After each day's prayer time, check off the box by each day's date.
Use the blanks to record any commitments, vows, or specific prayers
you want to remember.

Month_____Year_____

☐ 1._____
_____
_____

☐ 2._____
_____
_____

☐ 3._____
_____
_____

☐ 4._____
_____
_____

☐ 5._____
_____
_____

☐ 6._____
_____
_____

☐ 7._____
_____
_____

Prayer Diary

☐ 8._____

_____

_____

☐ 9._____

_____

_____

☐10._____

_____

_____

☐11._____

_____

_____

☐12._____

_____

_____

☐13._____

_____

_____

☐14._____

_____

_____

☐15._____

_____

_____

☐16._____

_____

_____

Prayer Diary

☐17._____
_____
_____

☐18._____
_____
_____

☐19._____
_____
_____

☐20._____
_____
_____

☐21._____
_____
_____

☐22._____
_____
_____

☐23._____
_____
_____

☐24._____
_____
_____

☐25._____
_____
_____

Prayer Diary

☐26._____
_____
_____

☐27._____
_____
_____

☐28._____
_____
_____

☐29._____
_____
_____

☐30._____
_____
_____

☐31._____
_____
_____

Prayer Diary

"Pray without ceasing."

—1 Thess. 5:17

After each day's prayer time, check off the box by each day's date. Use the blanks to record any commitments, vows, or specific prayers you want to remember.

Month_____Year_____

☐ 1._____

_____

_____

☐ 2._____

_____

_____

☐ 3._____

_____

_____

☐ 4._____

_____

_____

☐ 5._____

_____

_____

☐ 6._____

_____

_____

☐ 7._____

_____

_____

Prayer Diary

☐ 8._____
_____
_____

☐ 9._____
_____
_____

☐10._____
_____
_____

☐11._____
_____
_____

☐12._____
_____
_____

☐13._____
_____
_____

☐14._____
_____
_____

☐15._____
_____
_____

☐16._____
_____
_____

Prayer Diary

☐17._____
_____
_____

☐18._____
_____
_____

☐19._____
_____
_____

☐20._____
_____
_____

☐21._____
_____
_____

☐22._____
_____
_____

☐23._____
_____
_____

☐24._____
_____
_____

☐25._____
_____
_____

Prayer Diary

☐26._____
_____
_____

☐27._____
_____
_____

☐28._____
_____
_____

☐29._____
_____
_____

☐30._____
_____
_____

☐31._____
_____
_____

Prayer Diary

"Pray without ceasing."

—1 Thess. 5:17

After each day's prayer time, check off the box by each day's date.
Use the blanks to record any commitments, vows, or specific prayers
you want to remember.

Month_____Year_____

☐ 1._____

_____

_____

☐ 2._____

_____

_____

☐ 3._____

_____

_____

☐ 4._____

_____

_____

☐ 5._____

_____

_____

☐ 6._____

_____

_____

☐ 7._____

_____

_____

Prayer Diary

☐ 8._____

_____

_____

☐ 9._____

_____

_____

☐ 10._____

_____

_____

☐ 11._____

_____

_____

☐ 12._____

_____

_____

☐ 13._____

_____

_____

☐ 14._____

_____

_____

☐ 15._____

_____

_____

☐ 16._____

_____

_____

Prayer Diary

☐17. _____

_____

_____

☐18. _____

_____

_____

☐19. _____

_____

_____

☐20. _____

_____

_____

☐21. _____

_____

_____

☐22. _____

_____

_____

☐23. _____

_____

_____

☐24. _____

_____

_____

☐25. _____

_____

_____

Prayer Diary

☐26._____
_____
_____

☐27._____
_____
_____

☐28._____
_____
_____

☐29._____
_____
_____

☐30._____
_____
_____

☐31._____
_____
_____

Prayer Diary

"Pray without ceasing."

—1 Thess. 5:17

After each day's prayer time, check off the box by each day's date.
Use the blanks to record any commitments, vows, or specific prayers
you want to remember.

Month_____Year_____

☐ 1._____

_____

_____

☐ 2._____

_____

_____

☐ 3._____

_____

_____

☐ 4._____

_____

_____

☐ 5._____

_____

_____

☐ 6._____

_____

_____

☐ 7._____

_____

_____

Prayer Diary

☐ 8._____

_____

_____

☐ 9._____

_____

_____

☐10._____

_____

_____

☐11._____

_____

_____

☐12._____

_____

_____

☐13._____

_____

_____

☐14._____

_____

_____

☐15._____

_____

_____

☐16._____

_____

_____

Prayer Diary

☐17._____
_____
_____

☐18._____
_____
_____

☐19._____
_____
_____

☐20._____
_____
_____

☐21._____
_____
_____

☐22._____
_____
_____

☐23._____
_____
_____

☐24._____
_____
_____

☐25._____
_____
_____

Prayer Diary

☐26._____

_____

_____

☐27._____

_____

_____

☐28._____

_____

_____

☐29._____

_____

_____

☐30._____

_____

_____

☐31._____

_____

_____

Prayer Diary

"Pray without ceasing."

—1 Thess. 5:17

After each day's prayer time, check off the box by each day's date. Use the blanks to record any commitments, vows, or specific prayers you want to remember.

Month_____Year_____

☐ 1._____

_____

_____

☐ 2._____

_____

_____

☐ 3._____

_____

_____

☐ 4._____

_____

_____

☐ 5._____

_____

_____

☐ 6._____

_____

_____

☐ 7._____

_____

_____

Prayer Diary

☐ 8. _____
_____
_____

☐ 9. _____
_____
_____

☐10. _____
_____
_____

☐11. _____
_____
_____

☐12. _____
_____
_____

☐13. _____
_____
_____

☐14. _____
_____
_____

☐15. _____
_____
_____

☐16. _____
_____
_____

Prayer Diary

☐17._____

_____

_____

☐18._____

_____

_____

☐19._____

_____

_____

☐20._____

_____

_____

☐21._____

_____

_____

☐22._____

_____

_____

☐23._____

_____

_____

☐24._____

_____

_____

☐25._____

_____

_____

Prayer Diary

□26._____
_____
_____

□27._____
_____
_____

□28._____
_____
_____

□29._____
_____
_____

□30._____
_____
_____

□31._____
_____
_____

Prayer Diary

"Pray without ceasing."

—1 Thess. 5:17

After each day's prayer time, check off the box by each day's date. Use the blanks to record any commitments, vows, or specific prayers you want to remember.

Month_____ Year_____

☐ 1._____

_____

_____

☐ 2._____

_____

_____

☐ 3._____

_____

_____

☐ 4._____

_____

_____

☐ 5._____

_____

_____

☐ 6._____

_____

_____

☐ 7._____

_____

_____

Prayer Diary

☐ 8._____

_____

_____

☐ 9._____

_____

_____

☐10._____

_____

_____

☐11._____

_____

_____

☐12._____

_____

_____

☐13._____

_____

_____

☐14._____

_____

_____

☐15._____

_____

_____

☐16._____

_____

_____

Prayer Diary

☐17._____

_____

_____

☐18._____

_____

_____

☐19._____

_____

_____

☐20._____

_____

_____

☐21._____

_____

_____

☐22._____

_____

_____

☐23._____

_____

_____

☐24._____

_____

_____

☐25._____

_____

_____

Prayer Diary

□26._____

_____

_____

□27._____

_____

_____

□28._____

_____

_____

□29._____

_____

_____

□30._____

_____

_____

□31._____

_____

_____

Prayer Diary

"Pray without ceasing."

—1 Thess. 5:17

After each day's prayer time, check off the box by each day's date.
Use the blanks to record any commitments, vows, or specific prayers
you want to remember.

Month_____Year_____

☐ 1._____

_____

_____

☐ 2._____

_____

_____

☐ 3._____

_____

_____

☐ 4._____

_____

_____

☐ 5._____

_____

_____

☐ 6._____

_____

_____

☐ 7._____

_____

_____

Prayer Diary

☐ 8._____

_____

_____

☐ 9._____

_____

_____

☐ 10._____

_____

_____

☐ 11._____

_____

_____

☐ 12._____

_____

_____

☐ 13._____

_____

_____

☐ 14._____

_____

_____

☐ 15._____

_____

_____

☐ 16._____

_____

_____

Prayer Diary

□17._____

_____

_____

□18._____

_____

_____

□19._____

_____

_____

□20._____

_____

_____

□21._____

_____

_____

□22._____

_____

_____

□23._____

_____

_____

□24._____

_____

_____

□25._____

_____

_____

Prayer Diary

☐26._____
_____
_____

☐27._____
_____
_____

☐28._____
_____
_____

☐29._____
_____
_____

☐30._____
_____
_____

☐31._____
_____
_____

Prayer Diary

"Pray without ceasing."

—1 Thess. 5:17

After each day's prayer time, check off the box by each day's date.
Use the blanks to record any commitments, vows, or specific prayers
you want to remember.

Month_____Year_____

☐ 1._____

_____

_____

☐ 2._____

_____

_____

☐ 3._____

_____

_____

☐ 4._____

_____

_____

☐ 5._____

_____

_____

☐ 6._____

_____

_____

☐ 7._____

_____

_____

Prayer Diary

☐ 8._____

_____

_____

☐ 9._____

_____

_____

☐10._____

_____

_____

☐11._____

_____

_____

☐12._____

_____

_____

☐13._____

_____

_____

☐14._____

_____

_____

☐15._____

_____

_____

☐16._____

_____

_____

Prayer Diary

☐17._____
_____
_____

☐18._____
_____
_____

☐19._____
_____
_____

☐20._____
_____
_____

☐21._____
_____
_____

☐22._____
_____
_____

☐23._____
_____
_____

☐24._____
_____
_____

☐25._____
_____
_____

Prayer Diary

☐26._____

_____

_____

☐27._____

_____

_____

☐28._____

_____

_____

☐29._____

_____

_____

☐30._____

_____

_____

☐31._____

_____

_____

Prayer Diary

"Pray without ceasing."

—1 Thess. 5:17

After each day's prayer time, check off the box by each day's date. Use the blanks to record any commitments, vows, or specific prayers you want to remember.

Month_____Year_____

☐ 1._____
_____
_____

☐ 2._____
_____
_____

☐ 3._____
_____
_____

☐ 4._____
_____
_____

☐ 5._____
_____
_____

☐ 6._____
_____
_____

☐ 7._____
_____
_____

Prayer Diary

☐ 8._____
_____
_____
_____

☐ 9._____
_____
_____
_____

☐10._____
_____
_____
_____

☐11._____
_____
_____
_____

☐12._____
_____
_____
_____

☐13._____
_____
_____
_____

☐14._____
_____
_____

☐15._____
_____
_____

☐16._____
_____
_____

Prayer Diary

☐17._____

_____

_____

☐18._____

_____

_____

☐19._____

_____

_____

☐20._____

_____

_____

☐21._____

_____

_____

☐22._____

_____

_____

☐23._____

_____

_____

☐24._____

_____

_____

☐25._____

_____

_____

Prayer Diary

☐26._____
_____
_____

☐27._____
_____
_____

☐28._____
_____
_____

☐29._____
_____
_____

☐30._____
_____
_____

☐31._____
_____
_____

Prayer Diary

"Pray without ceasing."

—1 Thess. 5:17

After each day's prayer time, check off the box by each day's date.

Use the blanks to record any commitments, vows, or specific prayers

you want to remember.

Month_____Year_____

☐ 1._____

_____

_____

☐ 2._____

_____

_____

☐ 3._____

_____

_____

☐ 4._____

_____

_____

☐ 5._____

_____

_____

☐ 6._____

_____

_____

☐ 7._____

_____

_____

Prayer Diary

☐ 8._____

_____

_____

☐ 9._____

_____

_____

☐10._____

_____

_____

☐11._____

_____

_____

☐12._____

_____

_____

☐13._____

_____

_____

☐14._____

_____

_____

☐15._____

_____

_____

☐16._____

_____

_____

Prayer Diary

☐17._____

_____

_____

☐18._____

_____

_____

☐19._____

_____

_____

☐20._____

_____

_____

☐21._____

_____

_____

☐22._____

_____

_____

☐23._____

_____

_____

☐24._____

_____

_____

☐25._____

_____

_____

Prayer Diary

□26._____
_____
_____

□27._____
_____
_____

□28._____
_____
_____

□29._____
_____
_____

□30._____
_____
_____

□31._____
_____
_____

Prayer Diary

—1 Thess. 5:17

After each day's prayer time, check off the box by each day's date.
Use the blanks to record any commitments, vows, or specific prayers
you want to remember.

Month_____Year_____

□ 1._____

_____

_____

□ 2._____

_____

_____

□ 3._____

_____

_____

□ 4._____

_____

_____

□ 5._____

_____

_____

□ 6._____

_____

_____

□ 7._____

_____

_____

Prayer Diary

☐ 8._____
_____
_____

☐ 9._____
_____
_____

☐10._____
_____
_____

☐11._____
_____
_____

☐12._____
_____
_____

☐13._____
_____
_____

☐14._____
_____
_____

☐15._____
_____
_____

☐16._____
_____
_____

Prayer Diary

☐17._____

_____

_____

☐18._____

_____

_____

☐19._____

_____

_____

☐20._____

_____

_____

☐21._____

_____

_____

☐22._____

_____

_____

☐23._____

_____

_____

☐24._____

_____

_____

☐25._____

_____

_____

Prayer Diary

☐26._____

_____

_____

☐27._____

_____

_____

☐28._____

_____

_____

☐29._____

_____

_____

☐30._____

_____

_____

☐31._____

_____

_____

Answered Prayer

"Don't worry about anything; instead, pray about everything; tell God your needs and don't forget to thank him for his answers. If you do this you will experience God's peace, which is far more wonderful than the human mind can understand."

Philippians 4:6, 7, *The Living Bible*

Request *To grow Stronger with the Lord and be a Witness for the Lord.* Date *2-4-84*

Answer_____

_____ Date_____

Request *Steven And Teresa To go forward And Except The Lord* Date_____

Answer_____

_____ Date_____

Request_____

_____ Date_____

Answer_____

_____ Date_____

Request_____

_____ Date_____

Answer_____

_____ Date_____

Request_____

_____ Date_____

Answer_____

_____ Date_____

Request_____

_____ Date_____

Answer_____

_____ Date_____

Answered Prayer

Request_____

_____Date_____

Answer_____

_____Date_____

Request_____

_____Date_____

Answer_____

_____Date_____

Request_____

_____Date_____

Answer_____

_____Date_____

Request_____

_____Date_____

Answer_____

_____Date_____

Request_____

_____Date_____

Answer_____

_____Date_____

Request_____

_____Date_____

Answer_____

_____Date_____

Request_____

_____Date_____

Answer_____

_____Date_____

Answered Prayer

Request_____

_____Date_____

Answer_____

_____Date_____

Request_____

_____Date_____

Answer_____

_____Date_____

Request_____

_____Date_____

Answer_____

_____Date_____

Request_____

_____Date_____

Answer_____

_____Date_____

Request_____

_____Date_____

Answer_____

_____Date_____

Request_____

_____Date_____

Answer_____

_____Date_____

Request_____

_____Date_____

Answer_____

_____Date_____

Answered Prayer

Request_____

_____Date_____

Answer_____

_____Date_____

Request_____

_____Date_____

Answer_____

_____Date_____

Request_____

_____Date_____

Answer_____

_____Date_____

Request_____

_____Date_____

Answer_____

_____Date_____

Request_____

_____Date_____

Answer_____

_____Date_____

Request_____

_____Date_____

Answer_____

_____Date_____

Answered Prayer

Request_____
_____Date_____
Answer_____
_____Date_____
Request_____
_____Date_____
Answer_____
_____Date_____
Request_____
_____Date_____
Answer_____
_____Date_____
Request_____
_____Date_____
Answer_____
_____Date_____
Request_____
_____Date_____
Answer_____
_____Date_____
Request_____
_____Date_____
Answer_____
_____Date_____
Request_____
_____Date_____
Answer_____
_____Date_____

Answered Prayer

Request_____
_____Date_____
Answer_____
_____Date_____
Request_____
_____Date_____
Answer_____
_____Date_____
Request_____
_____Date_____
Answer_____
_____Date_____
Request_____
_____Date_____
Answer_____
_____Date_____
Request_____
_____Date_____
Answer_____
_____Date_____
Request_____
_____Date_____
Answer_____
_____Date_____
Request_____
_____Date_____
Answer_____
_____Date_____

Answered Prayer

Request_____

_____Date_____

Answer_____

_____Date_____

Request_____

_____Date_____

Answer_____

_____Date_____

Request_____

_____Date_____

Answer_____

_____Date_____

Request_____

_____Date_____

Answer_____

_____Date_____

Request_____

_____Date_____

Answer_____

_____Date_____

Request_____

_____Date_____

Answer_____

_____Date_____

Answered Prayer

Request_____
_____Date_____

Answer_____
_____Date_____

Request_____
_____Date_____

Answer_____
_____Date_____

Request_____
_____Date_____

Answer_____
_____Date_____

Request_____
_____Date_____

Answer_____
_____Date_____

Request_____
_____Date_____

Answer_____
_____Date_____

Request_____
_____Date_____

Answer_____
_____Date_____

Request_____
_____Date_____

Answer_____
_____Date_____